Central American Mythology

Captivating Myths of Gods, Goddesses, and Legendary Creatures of Ancient Mexico and Central America

© **Copyright 2019**

All Rights Reserved. No part of this book may be reproduced in any form without permission in writing from the author. Reviewers may quote brief passages in reviews.

Disclaimer: No part of this publication may be reproduced or transmitted in any form or by any means, mechanical or electronic, including photocopying or recording, or by any information storage and retrieval system, or transmitted by email without permission in writing from the publisher.

While all attempts have been made to verify the information provided in this publication, neither the author nor the publisher assumes any responsibility for errors, omissions or contrary interpretations of the subject matter herein.

This book is for entertainment purposes only. The views expressed are those of the author alone, and should not be taken as expert instruction or commands. The reader is responsible for his or her own actions.

Adherence to all applicable laws and regulations, including international, federal, state and local laws governing professional licensing, business practices, advertising and all other aspects of doing business in the US, Canada, UK or any other jurisdiction is the sole responsibility of the purchaser or reader.

Neither the author nor the publisher assumes any responsibility or liability whatsoever on the behalf of the purchaser or reader of these materials. Any perceived slight of any individual or organization is purely unintentional.

Free Bonus from Captivating History (Available for a Limited time)

Hi History Lovers!

Now you have a chance to join our exclusive history list so you can get your first history ebook for free as well as discounts and a potential to get more history books for free! Simply visit the link below to join.

Captivatinghistory.com/ebook

Also, make sure to follow us on Facebook, Twitter and Youtube by searching for Captivating History.

Contents

INTRODUCTION 1
OLOCUPINELE CREATES THE WORLD *(DULE/CUNA, PANAMA)*....... 3
WATAKAME' AND THE GREAT FLOOD *(WIXÁRITARI/HUICHOL, MEXICO)* 6
YOMUMULI AND THE TALKING TREE *(YOEME/YAQUI, MEXICO)*.... 11
HOW THE SEA WAS MADE *(CABÉCAR, COSTA RICA)* 14
MOTHER SCORPION'S COUNTRY *(MISKITO, NICARAGUA)* 17
THE CHILDHOOD OF THE SUN AND THE MOON *(QNE-A TNYA-E/CHATINO, MEXICO)* 21
THE INVISIBLE HUNTERS *(MISKITO, NICARAGUA)* 27
THE KING OF THE PECCARIES *(BRIBRI, COSTA RICA)*........................ 34
HOW OPOSSUM STOLE FIRE *(MAZATEC, MEXICO)* 37
UNCLE RABBIT AND UNCLE TIGER *(NICARAGUA)* 40
BIBLIOGRAPHY 46

Introduction

Mexico and the Central American states are home to many indigenous peoples, each of whom speaks their own language and lives according to their own customs. These diverse peoples have rich storytelling cultures, passing down myths about gods and the work of creation, and about the humans who for good or ill interact with these otherworldly beings. The loving god Olocupinele creates the world of the Cuna of Panama, while the goddess Nakawe' destroys and then remakes the world of the Huichol of Mexico. In the story "Mother Scorpion Country," from the Miskito of Nicaragua, we learn that even the goddess of the land of the dead cannot break the bond of love between a husband and wife.

Tricksters also figure in many tales told by indigenous peoples. Although tricksters sometimes cause harm, in the two trickster stories presented here, the tricksters use their wiles to help others. The opossum steals fire and brings it to the people in a Mazatec story from Mexico, while Uncle Rabbit saves his friend Bull from being eaten by Tiger in a story from Nicaragua.

Landscape and geography play vital roles in these stories, since ideas about how the world came to be are shaped by the place in which people live. Thus, the ocean figures prominently in creation stories from the Cuna of Panama and the Cabécar of Costa Rica, while life in a desert environment impacts the story "Yomumuli and the Talking Tree" from the Yaqui people, who live in northwestern Mexico and the southwestern United States.

For any culture, an important function of stories is to explain the origin of certain customs, to reinforce right behavior, and to discourage bad actions. We see this in several of the stories retold here. In the Miskito tale, "The Invisible Hunters," three brothers learn a hard lesson about keeping promises and the pitfalls of greed, while in "The King of the Peccaries" from the Bribri of Costa Rica, we receive instructions in ethical hunting practices. The origin of the Chatino tradition of parents bringing their newborn babies into a sweat bath to receive the blessings of the old grandmother is explained in the myth, "The Childhood of the Sun and Moon," and in "How the Sea Was Made," we get a brief glimpse into the burial customs of the Cabécar people of Costa Rica.

The stories presented in this volume are but a small sample of the abundant variety of myths and legends from Mexico and Central America. Nevertheless, they give us important glimpses into the ways people from this part of the world see themselves, as humans trying to understand their place within a larger universe containing beings both seen and unseen, and as people doing their best to live ethical lives that respect their fellow humans and the other creatures that live alongside them.

Note about tribal names: Where available, tribal names are given after the title of each story, along with the name of the country the people live in. Because names used by outsiders sometimes are different from the ones the people use to name themselves, I am giving first the name the people use and then the name that is more familiar to readers from outside those cultures. These are stated in the format "people's own name/attributed name, country." So, for example, the Huichol of Mexico call themselves *Wixáritari*, so their attribution would be "Wixáritari/Huichol, Mexico."

Olocupinele Creates the World (Dule/Cuna, Panama)

The Cuna people live in parts of the Isthmus of Panama, with some communities stretching south into what is now Colombia. Their primary deity is a being known as Olocupinele, who creates the world and everything in it. A striking feature of this myth is the insistence on love as the reason behind Olocupinele's act of creation.

Olocupinele it was who created the world. He created the Earth, the waters, the sky. He made a land that runs between two oceans. He gave the land hills and valleys, and on the land, he planted many trees and grasses and plants that are good for food. On the land, Olocupinele made animals to live. In the waters, he placed fish. In the skies, he placed birds. Olocupinele created clouds to make rain. He made refreshing pools of water and waterfalls and streams and rivers bearing water across the land and into the sea. And everything Olocupinele was made from his love. All creation comes from Olocupinele's dream, a dream of love.

Olocupinele also wanted to make people, beings like him. He wanted the people to have a good place to live. Olocupinele placed all manner of beautiful things in the world he had made: gemstones and precious metals, spices to flavor food, dyes to make bright cloth. All these he made and more, so that when the people came, they might have many good things, for Olocupinele loved the world he made, and he loved all his children.

Not until all was ready did Olocupinele create the people. Not until the mountains and valleys were green with trees and plants. Not until the birds and beasts and fish were thriving in their homes. Not until all the beautiful and useful things had been put in their places did Olocupinele create the people, and these people he called the Cuna.

The Cuna were made in the image of Olocupinele. He made men and women, beautiful and tall and strong. He gave to each of them a special gift. One was skilled in the hunt. One was the best maker of cloth. One was the best singer. One was the best dancer. Each of them had a special gift that they could share.

When the beautiful Cuna men and women were all created and given their gifts, Olocupinele put them on the Earth. The Cuna opened their eyes and found themselves in a bright garden. There were many beautiful trees, and the birds were all singing their songs. There were many good smells, of earth and rain and flowers. But the Cuna had never seen or heard or smelled any of this before, and they were frightened. The sun was too bright. The world was too green. The birds were too loud. The people hid themselves in the shadows.

Olocupinele looked upon his poor Cuna, who did not know how to live in the beautiful world he had made them, a world all made out of love. Then he decided to make one more Cuna man, a man he called Piler *(Pee-lair)*. To Piler, Olocupinele gave all manner of knowledge. Olocupinele sent Piler to the other Cuna, where they were hiding from the sun and the brightness of the world.

Piler went to the Cuna. He stood in the sunlight and laughed in delight. "Look!" he said. "Look at all the good things Olocupinele has made for us! Do not be afraid. This world is our home. There are so many good things here that Olocupinele has given us, and I will teach you how we should live. We must care for the Earth, always. We must care for each other, always. The Earth is ours to live in and to look after. Our Father Olocupinele says that this is what we are to do."

And so it was that the Cuna began to live in the place Olocupinele had made for them, the land between the two oceans, on the Earth made from a dream of love.

Watakame' and the Great Flood
(Wixáritari/Huichol, Mexico)

The Huichol people of west-central Mexico are known for their vibrant yarn paintings that depict myths and other stories and concepts that are important and sacred to them. Like many cultures throughout the world, the Huichol have a flood myth in which everything is destroyed and then remade anew.

Once there was a poor farmer named Watakame'. One day, he went out into his fields to work. He needed to clear a field of trees and bushes so that he could plant new crops. Watakame' took his sharp machete and chopped away at the trees, felling them. He chopped away at the bushes, felling them. It was very hard work, and at the end of the day, he was very tired. Watakame' went home, quickly ate a meal, and flopped down into his bed to sleep.

The next morning, Watakame' went out to chop down some more trees on the field he was clearing. When he arrived at the field, he couldn't believe his eyes: every tree and bush that he had chopped down the day before was back in its place, as if nothing had ever happened. He cut them down again and went home. For five days, this happened. Watakame' would clear part of the field, and in the morning, everything would be back the way it was.

"This cannot go on," said Watakame'. "If I cannot clear that field, I will not be able to plant, and if I cannot plant, I will have no crop to harvest, and I will starve. I must find out who is doing this to me."

In the morning, Watakame' went to the field as usual, but instead of going home at the end of the day, he hid himself to lie in wait for whoever or whatever was undoing all his hard work. Soon enough, an old woman appeared in the middle of the field. The old woman carried a long staff. Wherever she pointed with the staff, all the trees and bushes replanted themselves and came back to life.

Watakame' sprang out from the place he was hiding. "Aha!" he shouted. "You are the one who keeps undoing my work. Why do you do this? Do you not know that I will starve if I cannot plant my crops?"

"Oh, there are much worse things coming than starvation," said the old woman. "I am Nakawe', the goddess of the rain. I have come to tell you that the world will end soon. A great flood is coming that will cover the whole Earth, and it will not matter whether this field is cleared or not. The Sun has decided that the people on the Earth are too wicked, and he wants to kill them all and start over. But I have decided that I will save you, and save the animals, and that I will do the destruction myself."

"Tell me what I must do, Mother," said Watakame'. "I do not wish to drown."

"Do you know the place where the great fig tree grows?"

"Yes," said Watakame'. "I know it well."

"Cut down the fig tree, and use it to make a big box," said Nakawe'. "You must put yourself into the box. Take with you seeds of corn of all colors and beans of all colors. Take squash seeds, and your good black dog. Put a fire in your box, and keep it fed with squash stems. This must all be completed in five days."

Watakame' did what the goddess told him. He chopped down the fig tree and made a big box with it. He gathered the seeds and stems and a brazier to keep the fire in. On the fifth day, he put everything into the box, then climbed in with his dog. Nakawe' appeared and put the lid on the box. She caulked all the seams closed. Then Nakawe' called to her macaw. The goddess sat on top of the box with the macaw on her shoulder.

When all was ready, the wind began to blow. The wind howled through the trees. It roared through the valleys. It whipped around the mountaintops. Wherever the wind howled, the people were turned into animals. They became frightened and started fighting and killing each other. Soon, all the bad people were dead, and it was then that the sea began to rise. Up, up, up it climbed onto the land, filling the valleys, overtopping the hills, and finally covering even the highest mountain. Watakame' sat snugly inside his box with his dog, keeping the fire lit as the goddess had told him.

The box floated all around on the flood waters. It went east. It went west. It went north. It went south. The box went as far as it could go in each direction, measuring the breadth of the Earth. It took four years for the box to travel the whole Earth. In the fifth year, it rose straight up with the ever-rising waters, and it came down when the water started to recede. Finally, the box came to rest on the top of a mountain. Watakame' removed the lid of the box. He saw that the earth was all covered with water, except for the tip of the mountain where he was. But this didn't last long. The macaws and parrots were flying to and fro, digging new valleys and new channels for the water to run in so that the sea would return to its proper place and so that the Earth could dry out.

When all was ready, Nakawe' told Watakame' he could get out of his fig-wood box. "Use the seeds you brought with you to plant crops," she said. "Whenever you come home from your work, you will find tortillas prepared for you. I must go now, for I also have work to do, and in five days, all will be in readiness."

Watakame' did as Nakawe' told him to do. He tilled the soil and planted the seeds he brought with him. He found a cave for himself and his little dog to live in. Every evening when he came home from the fields, he found tortillas made for him. This was strange. He knew that Nakawe' was busy elsewhere, so who could have prepared this good food?

In five days, all was ready, as Nakawe' had promised. The Earth was full of new plants and animals. The trees were full of new birds. A whole new world had been made. Everything was fine and new and wonderful, except one thing: there were no people except Watakame', and he felt lonely.

On the sixth day, Nakawe' visited Watakame'. "Thank you for remaking the world so wonderfully," said Watakame'. "This is a good place to live. The soil is easy to till. My plants are growing quickly and well. The birds sing in the trees. And I have plenty to eat, but I do not understand where the food comes from. Is there someone else here with me? I should like to know, for I miss my family and my friends and would like some company."

Now, what had been happening was this: when Watakame' went to work in the fields, Nakawe' came to the cave. Nakawe' taught the dog how to transform herself into a woman. Then Nakawe' taught her how to cook and do other work that needed doing. And in the evening, when all was done and Watakame' was on his way home, the woman transformed herself back into a dog.

When Watakame' told Nakawe' that he wanted to know where the tortillas came from and that he was lonely, Nakawe' replied, "Tomorrow morning, instead of going to the fields to work, hide yourself somewhere about the cave. Watch what happens. You will know what to do."

Watakame' did what Nakawe' told him. He pretended to go out to the fields, but instead, he hid himself within the cave. As he looked, he saw the little dog rise out of her bed at the side of the cave. She slipped off her dog-skin and became a woman. The woman tended the fire and began preparing food.

Watakame' jumped out of his hiding place. He seized the dog-skin and threw it on the fire. The woman cried out in pain as though she was being burned. Her cries sounded like those of a dog. Watakame' then took the *masa*, the dough for making tortillas, that the woman had prepared. He threw it into the water she had set on the fire to boil, then he used this as medicine for the woman. He laved her whole body with it, and soon, she stopped crying and was healed. It was then that she turned into a real woman. She became Watakame''s wife. They were very happy together and had many children. And all the people in the world are the descendants of Watakame' and his wife.

Yomumuli and the Talking Tree (Yoeme/Yaqui, Mexico)

This Yaqui legend combines the myth about the creation of the world with Yaqui feelings about the Spanish Conquest, an event in history that led to much suffering and displacement of the Yaqui under colonial rule and later under the independent government of Mexico. The Yaqui people live in the northwestern Mexican state of Sonora and in the southwestern United States. They preserve many versions of this myth, but all of them center on the little Surem people and the humming tree or stick that tells the future.

There was a time when there were no people as there are today. The world was the way Yomumuli had made it. She made animals to live on the land and birds in the sky and fish in the waters, but instead of the tall people, she made the Surem. The Surem were little people, maybe only two or three feet high. They lived quite happily in their village.

In the center of the village was a large tree. One day, the tree began to hum. It hummed and vibrated and sometimes waved its branches gently. The Surem gathered around the tree, wondering why it was making these sounds. Surely there must be a reason, they thought, but they could not understand what the tree was saying to them.

The leader of the Surem spoke to the tree. "O Tree," he said, "we want to understand you. What are you saying?"

But the tree did not change its speech. It simply stood under the sky, humming.

The Surem tried many times to understand the tree and to speak to it, but nothing changed, until one day Yomumuli came to their village and said, "I understand what the tree is saying, and I will tell you if you will listen.

"This is what the tree is saying," Yomumuli said. "It is telling all the animals how they are to live. It says that some animals must eat plants. Some must eat other animals and birds. It is telling the waters what they must do, that the streams and rivers must flow downhill into lakes and into the sea."

"Oh!" said the Surem. "Those are wise sayings. Does the tree tell what will become of us?"

"Yes," said Yomumuli, "but you must believe that what I tell you is true, even though you will not like to hear it."

"Tell us anyway," said the Surem. "We will believe you."

"The tree says that the world will change. Strange people will come from far away. They will have many weapons. They will take away your lands and make you live according to their laws. They will make you worship their god. They will have many things all made of metal and many houses all made of stone."

"This is terrible!" cried the Surem. "Surely there are no such people in this world. Surely they will not come here. This cannot be what the tree says."

"Think what you like," said Yomumuli, although she was angry that the Surem did not believe her. But Yomumuli believed what the tree had said. She did not want to stay in the land of the Surem. She did not want to be there when the strange people from far away came to conquer everything and make the Surem worship their god.

Yomumuli went to the river. She rolled it up and took it away with her. Yomumuli walked ever northwards, away from the Surem, with her river tucked under her arm.

As for the Surem, many of them ran away from their village. Some went to live in the rivers and the sea, and the ones that did this turned into dolphins and whales. Some went to live under the hills or in the desert, and the ones that did this turned into ants. The Surem that stayed in their village grew very tall, and these became the Yaqui people.

It is said that if a Yaqui gets lost on the waters, the whales and dolphins will help them get home. And if a Yaqui gets lost in the hills or the desert, the Surem will help them there, too.

How the Sea Was Made *(Cabécar, Costa Rica)*

Costa Rica is a small Central American country with coastlines on both the Pacific Ocean and Caribbean Sea. This geographical reality is reflected in the Cabécar myth of the creation of the sea; the world starts out as a rock in the void, around which the sea eventually is created by the god Sibú, a deity the Cabécar share with the neighboring Bribri and Boruca tribes, and it is the presence of the new sea that allows Sibú to continue his work of creating a world with creatures in it.

This story also mentions Cabécar burial customs. Archaeologist Doris Stone reports that when someone has died among the Cabécar, their bodies are wrapped in the large leaves of the bijagua *(also known as the Cuban cigar plant), and this burial package is then covered with thorny material to prevent the body being disturbed by animals. Only when nothing but the clean bones are left is the body recovered and buried near the village.*

Before the world was made, there was only a great rock that stood in the middle of the void. Sibú the Creator thought to himself that there should be an Earth with people living on it and that maybe he could use the rock to make the Earth. Sibú knew that this would be a long and difficult task. He wanted someone to help him with it. He called to a woman named Sea and asked her to take a message to Thunder.

"Go to Thunder," said Sibú, "and tell him to come to me. I want to create an Earth with people on it, and I need his help and advice."

Sea went to Thunder and told him that Sibú wanted help creating the Earth and putting people on it, but Thunder refused to go. Sea went back to Sibú and told him that Thunder would not help.

"Maybe if I give Thunder my staff, he will help me," said Sibú. He gave the staff to Sea and told her to take it to Thunder. "Tell him that this is my good staff. He can use it to help him in his journey here to see me."

Sea took the staff to Thunder, but still he would not go to help Sibú. "Use the staff yourself on your journey back," said Thunder, "but take care not to misplace it. Never put it down, even for a moment."

Sea thought that Thunder's instructions were very odd, but she tried to obey them. But at one point in her journey, she did put the staff down, and when she went to pick it up again, she found that it had vanished. She looked for it everywhere. When she went to a patch of tall grass to see whether the staff was there, a venomous serpent darted out of the grass and bit her. A brief moment later, Sea was dead.

Sibú wondered what was taking Sea so long to return to him, so he went out searching for her. Soon, he came across her body. He prepared it for burial, wrapping it in *bijagua* leaves as is proper, but the body began to swell very strangely. Sibú put a frog on top of Sea's burial shroud to hold it in place, but when an insect flew by, the frog jumped up to snap at it. Sea's body continued to swell, growing larger and larger until it began to take a new shape. Her body became the trunk of a great tree. Her hair became leaves. All manner of bright birds began to nest among the leaves.

The tree grew and grew and grew. Finally, it became so tall that it pushed its way through the sky, which was where Sibú lived. "Oh!" said Sibú, "I do not want this tree inside my house! I must do something about this."

Sibú called to some birds. "Go to the top of the tree, and grab the branches at the top. Pull them around until they make a circle."

The birds went and did as Sibú commanded. They took the branches at the top of the tree and made a circle with them. When the circle was complete, the tree fell down and turned into water. The nests that were in the tree became turtles. The leaves of the tree became crabs. And everywhere around the rock that was in the void there was now water. Waves washed up onto the edge of the rock and crashed against it.

"There!" said Sibú when he saw the water the tree had become. "I have my house back. And now I can make an Earth and put people on it because now I have a sea with crabs and turtles in it."

And so Sibú made the Earth and put people on it, but to this day, the people know that the sound of the waves crashing on the shore is really the sound of the wind rushing through the leaves that were made out of Sea's hair.

Mother Scorpion's Country
(Miskito, Nicaragua)

The Miskito people live along the Caribbean coast of Nicaragua and were first contacted by the Spanish in the early sixteenth century. Later, many of the original Miskito people intermarried with black slaves who escaped from various Caribbean plantations. One result of this mixture of many cultures is that several languages are spoken by the Miskito: their indigenous tongue, Spanish, and a Miskito-English creole that resulted from contacts with British traders.

This legend about Mother Scorpion's country gives us insight into Miskito beliefs about the afterlife and about the loving bond between husband and wife.

Once there was a man named Nakili. He had a wife named Kati. They loved each other very much, and for a time, they lived happily together. But one day, Kati became very ill. Nakili cared for her as tenderly as he could and got her the best medicines he could find, but to no avail. After a few days, Kati died.

Every day, Nakili went to visit Kati's grave. He sat there, weeping many bitter tears and mourning her. He neglected his body and his work. One day, he arrived at the grave and saw the spirit of his dead wife hovering there.

"I am going to Mother Scorpion's country now," said the spirit.

"Oh, please, please, take me with you!" cried Nakili. "Don't leave me here all alone!"

"You cannot come with me," said Kati's spirit. "Mother Scorpion's country is the place for the shades of the dead. You are still a living man. You must stay here on the Earth."

Still Nakili begged and begged to be allowed to go with her, and finally, Kati gave in. "Follow me," she said and set off down the trail that led to Mother Scorpion's country. After they had walked a little way, they came to a place where there were many moths flying about in the air. The air was so thick with the little flying creatures that it was impossible to see what lay beyond them.

"Oh!" cried Kati. "I do not like this place. I am afraid of the moths. I do not want to have to walk through them."

"Have no fear," said Nakili. "I will make a path for us. Stay close to me."

And so, Nakili waded into the crowd of moths with Kati close beside him. Nakili waved his arms about, shooing the moths away, and soon, husband and wife had passed safely to the other side where there were no more moths.

They went a little farther until they came to the place where two great trees grew next to each other in the middle of the path. The trees were so close together that only Kati could pass between them. Nakili had to go around.

Next, they came to a gorge. At the bottom of the gorge was a lake of boiling water, and the only way across was a bridge that was so narrow and light that it looked like it was made from a single hair. Because Kati was a spirit, she was able to walk across the bridge, but Nakili knew he was too heavy to go that way. He looked from where he stood to the other side of the gorge and thought that perhaps he might be able to jump the gap. Nakili got a good running start then gave a great leap when he got to the edge of the gorge. He landed safely on the other side, where his wife's shade stood waiting for him.

Leaving the gorge behind them, husband and wife continued on their way. They walked for a very long time without encountering any other difficulties. Finally, they came to a wide river, the river that flows along the border of Mother Scorpion's country. Nakili and Kati paused on the banks of the river and looked across it. There, in Mother Scorpion's country, they could see the souls of the dead. Everyone on the other side of the river appeared to be happy.

Nakili and Kati looked about for a way to cross the river. Some way along the bank, they saw a canoe. In the canoe were four toads.

"Please," said Nakili to the toads, "can you take us to the other side of the river in your canoe?"

"With a good will," croaked the toads, "but our canoe cannot carry the body of a living person. That body is too heavy, and the canoe will capsize." So, Kati got into the canoe, and the toads began to paddle her across the river while Nakili swam alongside.

As they crossed, Kati looked into the water. "Oh!" she cried out, "the water is full of sharks! I am so frightened! Surely my husband will be devoured!"

Nakili looked about him in the water, but all he saw were small fish. "Never fear," he said. "Those are not sharks, just fish. I will not be harmed."

The toads looked over the side of their canoe and saw Nakili swimming there among the little fish. "Ah," said the chief toad, "you must be a good man. Because if you had been a wicked person, those fish would have turned into sharks and gobbled you right up!"

Soon, Nakili and the canoe arrived on the far bank of the river. Nakili helped his wife's spirit out of the canoe, and they both thanked the toads for their help. When both husband and wife were standing on the shore and the toads had gone back, a very tall, very stout woman came striding over to where Nakili and Kati stood. The woman had many breasts, from which the souls of the dead sometimes suckled. This was Mother Scorpion, and it was her country in which all the spirits of the good people lived after death.

"Welcome, my child," said Mother Scorpion to Kati. "Welcome to my country. Here you will have no pain or sorrow. You will always have plenty to eat, and you will not have to work. I am glad to receive you and for you to join my other children here."

Then Mother Scorpion turned to Nakili. She frowned angrily at him and said, "You, however, are not welcome. You are still alive. You should not be here. Go back to the land of the living where you belong!"

"Please, Mother Scorpion, let me stay!" begged Nakili. "I love Kati more than life itself, and I do not wish to be parted from her."

At first, Mother Scorpion would not listen to Nakili's pleas, but finally, she relented and let him stay.

For a time, Nakili and Kati lived very happily among the other souls, but one day, Nakili realized that he missed his children and wanted to see them again.

"I must go," Nakili said to Kati. "Mother Scorpion was right; I do not belong here. But one day I will come back, and we will never be parted again."

Nakili went to Mother Scorpion and told her that he wanted to go home to his children. Mother Scorpion cut down a big stalk of bamboo and put Nakili inside it, telling him that he must never return to her country until he had died himself. Then Mother Scorpion put the bamboo into the river, and it floated away.

After a time, Nakili realized that he was no longer on the river. He was being tossed about by waves. The river had emptied into the ocean, and now, the waves were carrying him back to the shore. Finally, the bamboo washed up onto the beach, and Nakili climbed out. He looked about and saw that he was standing in front of his own house, with his children running out to greet him.

The Childhood of the Sun and the Moon *(qne-a tnya-e/Chatino, Mexico)*

The Chatino people live in the state of Oaxaca in southern Mexico. This legend explains how the sun and moon got into the sky, and it also establishes the old woman who care for Sun and Moon during their childhood as the protector of newborn babies through the old woman's transformation into ashes in a sweat bath. According to author Lulu Delacre, Chatino parents still bring their newborn babies into a sweat bath that they might receive the protection of the old woman who cared for Sun and Moon when they were children.

There once was a time when the Sun and the Moon did not travel the sky but lived on the Earth as human beings. They were brothers, twins, and they walked about together as human brothers do.

One night, a Night Terror came upon the twins and tried to catch and eat them. Night Terror hated Sun and Moon because he was jealous of them. Sun and Moon ran from Night Terror. They ran until they came to a river. Sun and Moon plunged into the water and hid themselves there, hoping that Night Terror would not find them. But they had hidden near the mouth of the river, and when the tide of the ocean went out, the water of the river began to dry up. Night Terror was nearly upon the twins when an old woman passed by.

"Help us!" cried the children. "Night Terror is chasing us! He wants to kill and eat us!"

The old woman took pity on the children. She picked them up and put them in her mouth, one in each cheek. Her face became terribly swollen.

Once the children were safely hidden away, the old woman started walking back to her home. On her way, she met Night Terror.

"Have you seen two children anywhere near here?" said Night Terror.

"No, I haven't," said the woman.

Then Night Terror said, "Why is your head so big and round?"

"I have a terrible toothache," said the woman. "It has made my whole head swell up."

Night Terror believed the woman and went on its way, still hunting the children, not knowing that the old woman had fooled him by putting the twins in her cheeks.

When the old woman got home, she let the twins out of her cheeks. Since the children seemed to have no family, the old woman began to care for them herself. The children were very mischievous. The old woman could never finish her spinning properly because the boys would take the spindle and make a great tangle out of the thread. But the old woman was patient with them, and after a time, the children began to think that the old woman was their mother.

Sun and Moon lived happily with the old woman. They grew into fine, sturdy boys. They began to make their own bows and arrows, and when they had practiced using these, they went out into the forest to hunt for food. They often caught pigeons that they would bring home for the old woman to cook.

From time to time, the old woman would leave their home and go off into the forest. When the twins asked her where she was going, she always told them that she was going to visit her husband. Then one day, the twins asked her, "You are our mother, but who is our father?"

"My husband is your father," she replied.

"Why do we never see him?"

"Oh, he lives deep in the forest. He feels much happier and safer there," said the old woman. "But you must never see him, for I am afraid you might kill him."

The children became even more curious about their father after this, and so, they decided that the next time the old woman went to visit him they would follow her and see for themselves who their father was. Soon enough, the old woman announced that she was going to visit her husband. She told the children to stay at home and behave themselves.

"Yes, Mama," said the twins, but they had no intentions of staying behind. They secretly followed the old woman into the forest because they were determined to find out who their father was.

Deeper and deeper into the forest went the old woman, with Sun and Moon following after her. The children left behind them a trail of ashes so that they could find their way back out of the forest on their own. After a long time, they came to a little clearing where the old woman stopped and gave a strange cry. From their hiding place in the bushes, the children saw a great deer come into the clearing. The old woman greeted the deer and gave it some leaves and grass she had brought with her.

As soon as the children saw the old woman feed the deer, they followed the trail of ashes back to the house. They arrived there before the old woman and pretended that they had never left.

Some days later, the old woman asked the children to mow some fresh grass for her to take to her husband. The children fashioned a scythe out of wood and went into a meadow where there was a quantity of long, green grass. Sun took the scythe and swung it with great speed and force. It sliced through the grass very easily, but it frightened a young rabbit that had hidden itself in the grass. The rabbit leapt up out of the grass and hit Moon in the face so hard that an imprint of its body remained there, and this is why we can see the shape of a rabbit in the moon even today.

The next day, the twins decided they would go to the clearing and see whether they might meet their father for themselves. They followed the trail of ashes, and when they got to the clearing, they called out in the same way they had heard the old woman do. Soon enough, a great deer came into the clearing.

"This can't possibly be our father," said Sun to Moon. "It is such an ugly creature."

"Yes," said Moon. "Look at its great spindly legs. It looks quite out of proportion."

The twins decided to kill the deer. They shot it through the heart with their arrows, and when it was dead, they skinned it and took out its organs. They set aside the liver to take home to the old woman but used some of the other organs to make a dish called *skualyku*. They cooked it right there in the clearing and ate it all up. Then they took the empty deer hide, filled it full of wasps, and sewed it shut. They left the wasp-filled hide there on the floor of the clearing, and it looked like the deer was lying there, asleep.

When the children were done eating and sewing up the deer hide, they took the liver back to the old woman. She thanked them for their gift and prepared to eat it. Just as she was about to bite into the liver, it cried out, and a nearby frog started to sing, "You are eating your husband, you are eating your husband." It sang that song three times.

Then the old woman looked at the children. "Is this true? Did you kill my husband?"

"Of course not!" said the children. "Frogs never know what they are talking about. You shouldn't listen to them."

But the old woman's suspicions were not allayed. She went to the clearing where she saw the deer hide on the forest floor. She thought that her husband was being lazy, and this made her angry. The old woman took her staff and began beating the deer hide. She hit it so hard that the seams split wide open, and hundreds of angry wasps swarmed out. They attacked the old woman, stinging her all over her body.

Screaming in pain, the old woman ran back home. She ran past the field that the children had mown the other day. The baby rabbit called out to her as she went by. "Jump in the water! Jump in the water!" said the rabbit.

"No, that will not help," said the old woman. "I need my children to make a sweat bath for me."

When the woman arrived home, the children saw that she was covered in wasp stings. They lit a huge fire and put many medicinal plants in it so that it would make a healing smoke to soothe her wounds. The old woman sat before the fire. At first, she started feeling better, but then she felt too hot. "Children, please take me out of the sweat bath," she said.

"No, Mama, we cannot do that," said the children. "You must stay there. This is how you will become the protector of all new children."

The old woman stayed in the sweat bath. She became so hot that she burned up into ashes. Once they saw that the old woman was nothing but ashes, the children took up the old woman's staff and a skein of her thread then left their home and started climbing into the hills.

While they were climbing, Sun turned to Moon and said, "I am feeling very sad. Our mother had to live and die in a world without light. I wonder what we could do to honor her now that she is dead."

Moon said, "I know what we could do. We could climb to the very highest mountain we can find. We could shine our light on her from there."

Sun agreed that this was a good plan, so they started walking up the highest mountain they could find. On their way up, they came across a great serpent that had glowing eyes. The children looked at it for a moment then decided to kill the serpent. Sun hit the serpent with the staff. Moon strangled it with some of the thread. And when the serpent was dead, the children took out its eyes. Moon kept the right eye, which was the brightest one. Sun kept the duller, left eye.

Up, up, up the mountain the children climbed. Presently, they came upon a hollow tree that had a beehive in it. Moon took some of the honey and ate it. It was very good and very sweet, but it made him very thirsty indeed. Sun took the old woman's staff and drove it into the ground. Where the staff entered the soil, a spring of water spurted out.

"Give me some of that water to drink," said Moon. "I am terribly thirsty after eating all that honey."

"I will not give you any water unless you trade your serpent's eye for the one that I have," said Sun.

Moon was angry that Sun would do something like this because he wanted to keep the brighter eye. But in the end, he traded with Sun because he could no longer stand how thirsty he had become. And this is why the Sun is brighter than the Moon.

Up, up, up the children climbed, until they reached the very top of the mountain peak. Sun took the skein of thread and threw one end into the sky. The thread made a path for the children to follow into the heavens. Sun went first because he had the brighter serpent's eye and could see the way more easily. Moon followed Sun with his lesser serpent's eye. When they arrived up in the heavens, they started their travels across the sky.

And this is how Sun and Moon came to be in the heavens and how light came to be on the Earth.

The Invisible Hunters *(Miskito, Nicaragua)*

In the legend of the invisible hunters, three Miskito men learn a hard lesson about greed. This cautionary tale also bears the imprint of indigenous Miskito contact with Europeans since the goods offered by the traders seem to be European products and the hunters must make a choice between their traditional manner of hunting with spears or using modern firearms, which were introduced by European colonizers.

Once there were three brothers who lived in the village of Ulwas on the Coco River. They were very good hunters. They never failed to come back from their hunt with something to share with the rest of the village. One day, they decided to go hunting for *wari*, a kind of wild pig that has the most delicious meat of any animal in the forest. The brothers took up their spears and went out into the forest. They walked for a long time, not seeing any wari at all.

Suddenly, they heard a strange voice. "Dar, dar, dar," said the voice.

"Did you say that?" asked the eldest brother.

"No, we did not speak at all," said the other two.

The brothers waited for a moment to see whether they might spy on who or what the voice belonged to, but all they heard were the usual forest sounds.

As soon as they started to go back to their hunt, they heard the voice again. "Dar, dar, dar," it said.

"Did you say that?" asked the youngest brother.

"No, we did not speak at all," said the other two.

They looked around them and saw a vine swinging from a tree nearby. "Dar, dar, dar," said the vine.

The three brothers went over to the tree where the vine was swinging. The first brother took hold of the vine, and suddenly, he disappeared! Then the second brother also took hold of the vine, and he disappeared as well. The youngest brother was very frightened indeed. "Give me back my brothers!" he shouted at the vine.

"I haven't taken them anywhere," said the vine. "They're right here in front of you. All they need to do is let go of me, and you will be able to see them again."

The two invisible brothers let go of the vine, and suddenly, they reappeared. The three brothers looked at the vine in wonder. "Who are you?" they said.

"I am the Dar, and whoever touches me becomes invisible to others. Neither humans nor animals will be able to see you at all."

The brothers thought about what the Dar had said.

"If we each take a piece of this vine," said the eldest, "we will be the greatest hunters in the world. We will be able to stalk any animal we want."

"Yes," said the second brother. "Let us each take a piece of the vine. Let us do that now."

The brothers all lunged for the vine, but it swung far out of their reach and disappeared. Then the brothers heard the voice of the Dar again. "I will let you take me," it said, "but first you must promise me two things."

"Very well," said the brothers. "You have our word."

"First, you must never sell the wari meat. You must give it away to those who need it. Second, you must never use guns in your hunt. You must use only spears."

"We promise," said the brothers. "We will do exactly as you say."

Then the Dar reappeared and swung down in front of the brothers. The Dar allowed each of them to cut off a small piece with their knives. The rest of the Dar then vanished, and the brothers continued on their hunt.

That day, they took many, many wari. Before they left for home, they returned their pieces of the Dar to the tree where they had found the vine. They left the pieces of vine on a branch of the tree. Then they brought the wari back to their village and gave the meat away to everyone who needed food.

The people in Ulwas were astonished to see so many wari killed in a single hunt. Soon, they had skinned and cleaned the animals, and then they cooked them and ate them in a great feast. Everyone was very happy and very content when the meal was done.

After the meal, the village elders summoned the brothers. "We would like to know how you had such great fortune in the hunt. Never has anyone brought back so many wari on the same day."

"We went into the forest the way we often do," said the eldest brother, "and then we heard a voice. It was the Dar, a magical vine that makes things invisible. After we promised to hunt only with spears and to give the meat away, the Dar let us each take a little piece of itself, and so, we became invisible to the wari. That is how we caught so many."

"Ah!" said the elders. "That is truly good fortune. The legend of the Dar is very, very old. You were very lucky to have found it. But be sure you keep your promises to it!"

It was not long before the fame of the brothers from Ulwas had spread up and down the Coco River. One day, a boat full of strangers arrived in Ulwas. The boat carried a cargo of well-woven cloth and barrels of wine.

"Greetings to you!" said the strangers. "We have come from far away to meet the famous hunters from Ulwas. We have come to trade you our fine cloth and our good wine for some wari meat."

"We cannot sell the meat to you," said the second brother. "Our people need it for food."

"Of course they do!" said the strangers. "We only want to buy the portion they do not need."

The brothers stood aside to talk about what the strangers had said.

"Maybe we could sell just a little bit," said the eldest brother.

"No, we should not do that," said the second brother. "We made a promise to the Dar. Surely it will know if we have not kept our word."

"Yes, we did promise," said the youngest brother, "but surely these traders also have power since they can make such fine cloth and so many barrels of wine. Maybe they are more powerful than the Dar."

The other brothers thought about what the youngest one had said and agreed with him. They went to the traders and exchanged wari meat for cloth and wine. The traders left the village, apparently content with the exchange.

It was not long before the traders came back with more cloth and more wine to trade for wari meat. This they did many times, making bigger and bigger exchanges, until finally the brothers realized that they were trading too much. Soon there would not be enough meat to feed the people.

One day, the traders arrived with more cargo to trade. The three brothers met them at the riverbank. "We can no longer trade with you," said the eldest brother. "We do not have enough meat to feed the people."

"That is because you only hunt with spears," said the traders. "If you used guns, you would be able to kill more wari more quickly, and then you'd have enough both to feed your village and to trade with us."

The brothers decided that what the traders had said was wise. They bought guns and used those to hunt in the forest. With the guns, they were able to kill enough wari both to satisfy the traders and to feed the people. And the brothers no longer gave any thought to their promise to the Dar.

Again and again, the traders came back. Always they brought rich things to trade for the wari meat. The brothers greedily took whatever the traders brought, and soon, they found that there was not enough meat to satisfy both the traders and the hunger of the village.

The village elders watched what the brothers were doing and became concerned. They called the brothers before them to account for their deeds. "You are trading too much," said the elders. "Our people are going hungry while you become rich with the traders' wares."

"Well," said the brothers, "if the people want to get more meat from us, maybe they should pay for it like the traders do."

But the people of Ulwas were poor people. They did not have finely woven cloth. They did not have barrels of wine. They had no money to trade for the meat.

One day, the brothers returned from the hunt to find the people of the village waiting for them at the end of the path.

"Give us the meat," said the people.

"Pay us for it then," said the brothers.

"We cannot pay," said the people. "We are poor villagers."

So, the brothers gave the villagers the bad parts of the meat which they knew the traders would not take. The people became very angry at this, but the brothers only laughed at them and went about their business.

For many months, the brothers continued to hunt with guns and sold what they had caught to the traders. The people of the village became ever more hungry because the brothers would not share their catch with them.

One day, the brothers returned from their hunt laden with wari. But as they came to the entrance to the village, the assembled people did not run up to them and beg for meat. Instead, they all screamed and ran away because they saw only a line of dead wari floating along through the air by themselves. The elders heard the commotion and went out to see what was wrong. "Ah!" they said. "The Dar has made the hunters invisible."

The brothers halted in their tracks when the people started running away from them. Then they looked at each other. Nothing could they see but the dead wari floating in the air.

"What has happened?" asked the eldest brother.

"We left our pieces of the Dar on the tree like we always do," said the second.

"We are still invisible, just the same!" said the youngest. "Oh, this is very, very bad."

They dropped the dead wari there on the path and raced back to the Dar's tree where they fell on their knees. "What has happened to us?" they cried. "Why are we still invisible?"

But the Dar did not answer them, no matter how they begged for mercy. The only thing it said was "Dar, dar, dar, dar," over and over.

"We have done this to ourselves," said the brothers. "We did not keep our promise to the Dar. We were greedy and treated our people very badly. We must go back to our village and beg forgiveness of the elders and the people."

The brothers went back to the village. They went down on their knees before the elders and begged for forgiveness. But the elders would not forgive them for what they had done. Instead, they banished the invisible hunters from the village forever.

The invisible hunters went back into the forest. They wandered up and down the river, looking for the Dar and begging it to make them visible again. Some say that the brothers wander there still, for hunters on the trail sometimes swear that they have heard three tearful voices crying out, "Dar, dar, dar."

The King of the Peccaries *(Bribri, Costa Rica)*

An important part of indigenous subsistence is hunting the animals and birds that live near human settlements. This legend from the Bribri people of Costa Rica concerns itself with ethical hunting of animals for food. In this cautionary tale, the unskilled hunter who falls afoul of the King of the Peccaries does pay a price but only a temporary one: the King's goal is instruction and reform of the hunter's ways, not revenge.

One day, two Bribri hunters went out with their bows and arrows to see what they might catch to eat. They walked quietly through the forest, bows at the ready, in case they saw an animal or bird. For a long time, they crept along the forest path, not seeing anything, until one of them spied a peccary. He let fly with his arrow, but he did not shoot well. The animal was hit, but it was only wounded. The peccary bounded off into the forest, and the hunter ran after it. The hunter's companion soon lost sight of both his friend and their prey. Eventually, he gave up looking and went back home, thinking that his friend would come home when he had caught and killed the peccary.

But the first hunter did not come home. He chased after the peccary, going deeper and deeper into the forest, but no matter how quickly he ran, the peccary went even faster, and soon, the animal was lost to sight. The hunter decided to give up the chase. While he was resting and catching his breath before returning home, a man appeared before him. The man was very tall and very stately. He had fine black hair and was dressed very well.

"Follow me," said the tall man, who then strode off toward another part of the forest.

The hunter thought it wise to go with this man since he seemed to be very powerful. He followed the tall man through the forest until they came to a large house.

"This is my home," said the tall man. "Please come in."

The hunter went into the house and saw that it was very finely built and beautifully decorated and furnished with many well-made hammocks. But the most surprising thing is that the house was also full of animals of all kinds, and every one of them seemed happy and very well cared for.

"Do you see all these animals here in my house?" said the tall man. "These are my subjects, for I am the King of the Peccaries. When hunters wound animals but do not kill them, the animals come to me to be healed, or else I find them in the forest and bring them here. But if they cannot be healed, I use them for food for myself and my guests.

"Listen to me," said the King, "and listen well: when you go into the forest to hunt, you must do that duty very, very well. It is not right to shoot at an animal and leave it wounded without killing it. You must try to kill the beast with the very first shot. That is the proper way to do things."

"That is what I shall do, always, from now on," said the hunter. "I did not know how much harm I was doing before. I shall change my ways."

"That is very good," said the King. "Now, come here and have a seat, and eat and drink. You have had a long and weary day, and you need refreshment before you can go home."

The hunter sat in the place the King prepared for him and ate of the peccary he had wounded earlier, which the King had found and then killed and cooked. The King also served good maize beer to his guest.

When the meal was done, the hunter said, "I thank you, O King of the Peccaries, for my meal and for my lesson. I will try to do as you ask and be a better hunter."

"This I know you will do," said the King. "But there is yet a price to be paid for your error." He handed a piece of cane to the hunter. "You must take this back to your home and plant it in front of your house. You will not be able to speak until the cane has fully grown. And when the cane is grown, you must tell all your people what happened to you, and give them my instructions about hunting."

The hunter thanked the King once more, then took the piece of cane and returned home. He did as the King of the Peccaries had instructed him, planting the cane in front of his house. The hunter could not speak until the cane was fully grown, and when it was, he told all the village what had happened to him.

How Opossum Stole Fire *(Mazatec, Mexico)*

The trope of an animal using its tail to bring fire to people is common to many cultures. In James George Frazer's book of fire-origin myths from around the world, animals as varied as snakes, dogs, and hummingbirds use their tails to bring fire to the people. In this trickster myth from the Mazatec people of Oaxaca, Mexico, the fire-bringer is the opossum, and he pays for his trick by losing all the fur on his tail.

A long time ago, fire did not exist on the Earth. Fire only was found in the sun and the stars. One day, some fire fell from the heavens onto the Earth. An old woman saw it fall. She went to where the fire fell and collected some up. She brought it home with her, placed it in her hearth, and tended it with care. The people saw that the old woman had fire. They asked whether she might share it with them, but she always refused. She wanted to keep the fire for herself alone.

And so it was that all the people were cold and had no way to cook their food. Again and again, they asked the old woman to share her fire, but every time they asked, she told them to go away. This made the people very sad indeed.

One day, an opossum ambled by a village of people. He saw that the people were all very cold and were eating uncooked food. He also saw that they were very sorrowful.

"Greetings, cousins," said the opossum. "What is it that makes you so very sad?"

"We do not have fire to keep us warm or to cook our food. The old woman has some, but she won't share it with us. That is why we are sad," said the people.

"If I went and stole some fire for you, would you promise not to hunt and eat me?" said the opossum.

The people looked at the little opossum and burst into laughter, but the opossum was not bothered by it. "I know you think I am quite amusing," he said, "but I will do as I said I would. I will steal fire for you."

When night fell, the opossum visited all the houses of the people. He told each household that he was going to steal fire for them so they needed to be ready and waiting for his return.

The opossum went to the old woman's house where he found her sitting before her hearth. On the hearth was a large fire, merrily blazing away. "Greetings, mother," said the opossum. "How fortunate you are to have a fire! It is so cold outside I am sure it will be the death of me. Can I sit by your fire with you and warm myself?"

The old woman looked down at the small, shivering opossum and felt sorry for him. "Yes, indeed," she said. "You may sit by my fire and warm yourself with me."

The opossum sat down a little distance from the fire. Bit by bit, he inched closer and closer to the hearth. Because he only moved a little at a time, the old woman didn't notice what he was doing. Now, it is important to remember that at this time the opossum had a fine, furry tail, much like a fox or a squirrel. Soon, the opossum got close enough to touch the fire. He took his fine, furry tail and put it into the flames. Instantly, the opossum went running out of the old woman's house, his tail ablaze.

The old woman was furious. She tried to chase the opossum, but he was too quick for her. The opossum ran back to the village with his burning tail. He gave some of the fire to each of the households until finally the fire was spent. All the fine fur on the opossum's tail was singed quite away, and that is why today opossums have naked tails.

Uncle Rabbit and Uncle Tiger (Nicaragua)

Animal tales are common to cultures the world over, and Central America has its share of these fun stories. One character that commonly appears in their animal tales is wily Uncle Rabbit, the primary trickster in stories widely told in both Costa Rica and Nicaragua, stories that are not confined to one particular indigenous group. This story about Uncle Rabbit's victory over Uncle Tiger comes from Nicaragua, and it is a cautionary tale about helping harmful and ungrateful people.

Tiger was walking down the path on a very windy day. How the wind howled through the trees! Even Tiger could not roar so loudly. But Tiger didn't pay the wind any mind until suddenly a large branch was blown off a tree. The branch landed right on top of Tiger. The branch was so heavy that Tiger couldn't move.

"Oh, dear, oh, dear," said Tiger. "I shall never get free. I shall be stuck here forever, and I shall die of hunger and thirst."

As Tiger lay under the branch lamenting his predicament, Bull came trotting down the same path. He was hurrying to get home because he did not like the wind one bit.

Tiger heard Bull and called out, "Uncle Bull! Uncle Bull! Oh, come quickly and help me! I am trapped here under this branch, and I cannot get out."

Bull went over to Tiger and said, "Oh, my. You are stuck indeed. But maybe I shouldn't help you, for surely as soon as you are free, you will leap on me and eat me."

"I promise with all my heart that I will not eat you," said Tiger. "Please lift the branch so that I can go free."

"You promise?" said Bull.

"I promise. I swear most solemnly," said Tiger.

"Very well," said Bull. "I'll help you. But don't you forget your promise!"

Bull put his horns under the branch. With his strong neck, he tossed the heavy branch aside. But as soon as Tiger was free, he leapt upon Bull and started biting him.

"Tiger!" said Bull. "You promised! You said you would not eat me!"

"Well, I'm hungry," said Tiger. "And you look so very tasty. But I'll stop for now. Instead, we'll go along the path and ask for advice. We'll see whether anyone agrees that I should eat you or whether they think I should let you go free. We will abide by the judgement of whoever makes the best argument."

"Very well," said Bull, and so they set off down the path.

Soon enough, they came across a very old Ox.

"Uncle Ox," said Tiger, "we need your advice. If someone does a good deed, how do they get repaid?"

Ox scoffed. "Not with kindness, that's certain," he said. "Look at me. I worked and worked and worked for a farmer. I pulled his plow year after year. I worked so hard, but when I became feeble, he sent me away instead of caring for me in my old age. I did so many good deeds for him, but he only repaid me with a bad one."

Tiger and Bull bade Ox farewell and continued down the path. "Ha!" said Tiger. "We already found one person who agrees with me. I wonder what the next one will say?"

Soon enough, Tiger and Bull came upon a very old Horse.

"Uncle Horse," said Tiger, "we need your advice. If someone does a good deed, how do they get repaid?"

"Well, all you need to know to answer your question is to look at me," said Horse. "I worked so very, very hard for the man who owned me. I carried him everywhere on my back. I pulled his cart. I pulled his plow. I carried his children. Every night he would go out drinking, and I would carry him home safely when he was too drunk to stand. But now that I am old and feeble, he has turned me out of my stable instead of caring for me. I did so many good deeds for him, but he only repaid me with a bad one."

Tiger and Bull bade Horse farewell and continued down the path. "Ha!" said Tiger. "That's two people who agree with me!"

Bull began to feel very afraid. If the next person also agreed with Tiger, surely Tiger would eat him all up.

Tiger and Bull continued down the path. Suddenly, Rabbit jumped out in front of them.

"Uncle Rabbit," said Tiger, "we need your advice. If someone does a good deed, how do they get repaid?"

"Hmmm," said Rabbit. "That's an important question. And a difficult one. What kind of good deed did you have in mind?"

Bull said, "Today I was walking down the path, and I came across Uncle Tiger. He was trapped underneath a very heavy branch. He asked me to help him out, so I did. And now he wants to eat me. So, we're asking for advice about whether he should do that or not."

"Oh, that is a difficult question," said Rabbit, "but I'm not sure I understand what happened. Can you explain it again?"

This time Tiger told Rabbit how Bull had freed him.

"Yes, but I still don't understand how Bull managed to set you free. I think I need to see what happened. Can you take me to the place where the branch is?"

Tiger, Bull, and Rabbit went back to the place where Tiger had been trapped under the branch.

"Oh, that is a very large branch," said Rabbit, "but I still don't understand how you could have been trapped by it. Lie down in the path. Then Bull can put the branch back on top of you, and then he can show me how he pushed it away. Then I'll understand, and I'll be able to answer your question."

Tiger lay down in the middle of the path. Bull picked up the branch with his horns and put it back on top of Tiger.

"Now we run!" Rabbit said to Bull, and the two of them ran away, leaving Tiger trapped once again and roaring with anger at having been tricked.

When Rabbit and Bull were safely away, Rabbit said to Bull, "Don't go back there. And think twice before helping someone who is likely to harm you."

Here's another book that I think you'd be interested in:

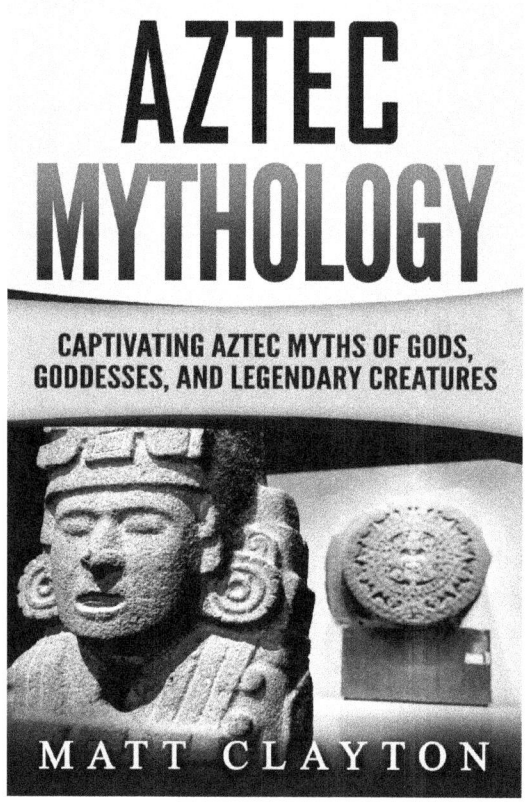

And another one...

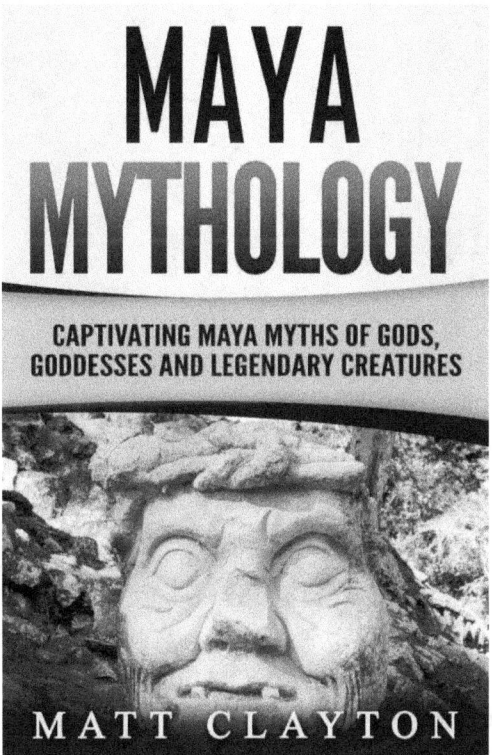

Bibliography

Bierhorst, John, ed. *The Deetkatoo: Native American Stories About Little People*. New York: William Morrow and Company, Inc., 1998.

———. *The Mythology of Mexico and Central America*. New York: William Morrow and Company, Inc., 1990.

Conzemius, Eduard. "Ethnographical Survey of the Miskito Indians of Nicaragua and Honduras." *Smithsonian Institution Bureau of American Ethnology, Bulletin 106*. Washington, DC: United States Government Printing Office, 1932.

Delacre, Lulu. *Golden Tales: Myths, Legends, and Folktales from Latin America*. New York: Scholastic, Inc., 1996.

Endrezze, Anita. *Throwing Fire at the Sun, Water at the Moon*. Tucson: University of Arizona Press, 2000.

Evers, Larry, ed. *The South Corner of Time: Hopi, Navajo, Papago, Yaqui Tribal Literature*. n. c.: University of Arizona Press, 1980.

Fabrega, H. Pittier de. "Folk-Lore of the Bribri and Brunka Indians in Costa Rica." *Journal of American Folk-lore* 16 (1903): 1-9.

Foss, Flora. *World Myths and Legends II: Mexico*. Belmont: Fearon/Janus/Quercus, 1993.

Frazer, Sir James George. *Myths of the Origin of Fire: An Essay*. London: Macmillan and Co., Ltd., 1930.

Friesen, Alyssa. "The Legend of the Miskito Indians: A Literary Translation Project." *SWOSU Journal of Undergraduate Research* 2 (2018): 24-34.

Giddings, Ruth Warner. *Yaqui Myths and Legends*. Anthropological Papers of the University of Arizona 2. Tucson: [University of Arizona Press], 1959.

Love, Hallie N. *Watakame's Journey: The Story of the Great Flood and the New World*. Santa Fe: Clear Light Publishers, 1999.

Loya, Olga. *Momentos Magicos/Magic Moments: Tales from Latin America Told in English and Spanish*. Little Rock: August House Publishers Inc., 1997.

Lumholtz, Carl. "Symbolism of the Huichol Indians." *Memoirs of the American Museum of Natural History* 3 (1907): 1-228.

Nava, Yolanda. *It's All in the Frijoles: 100 Famous Latinos Share Real-Life Stories, Time-Tested Dichos, Favorite Folktales, and Inspiring Words of Wisdom*. New York: Simon & Schuster, 2000.

Pittier, H. Fabrega de. "The Folk-Lore of the Bribri and Brunka Indians in Costa Rica." *The Journal of American Folk-Lore* 16 (1903): 1-9.

Porras, Tomas Herrera. *Cuna Cosmology: Legends from Panama*. Trans. Anita McAndrews. Washington, DC: Three Continents Press, 1978.

Harriet Rohmer, Octavio Chow, Morris Viduare, Rosalma Zubizarreta, and Alma Flor Ada. *The Invisible Hunters/Los Cazadores Invisibles: A Legend from the Miskito Indians of Nicaragua*. n.c.: n.p., 1987.

Sáenz, Adela de Ferreto, *La Creacion de la tierra y otras historias del buen Sibú y de los Bribris*. San Jose, Costa Rica: Editorial Universidad Estatal a Distancia, 1982.

Schmitt, Martha. *World Myths and Legends II: Central America*. Belmont: Fearon/Janus/Quercus, 1993.

Stone, Doris. *The Talamancan Tribes of Costa Rica*. Cambridge, MA: The Peabody Museum, 1962. Repr. 1973.

Suárez-Rivas, Maite. *Latino Read-Aloud Stories*. New York: Black Dog & Leventhal Publishers, 2000.

Zingg, Robert M. *Huichol Mythology*. Tucson: University of Arizona Press, 2004.

www.ingramcontent.com/pod-product-compliance
Lightning Source LLC
Chambersburg PA
CBHW070049230426
43661CB00005B/836